Nelson

Handwriting

Resources and Assessment

BOOK 1 AND BOOK 2

Anita Warwick

Series editor: John Jackman

Original authors: Louis Fidge and Peter Smith

OXFORD
UNIVERSITY PRESS

OXFORD
UNIVERSITY PRESS

Great Clarendon Street, Oxford, OX2 6DP, United Kingdom

Oxford University Press is a department of the University of Oxford. It furthers the University's objective of excellence in research, scholarship, and education by publishing worldwide. Oxford is a registered trade mark of Oxford University Press in the UK and in certain other countries

First published by Nelson Thornes Ltd in 2003
This edition published by Oxford University Press in 2014

British Library Cataloguing in Publication Data
Data available

978-0-7487-7006-9

15

Printed in Great Britain

Acknowledgements

Cover: Lisa Smith
Logo: Woody Fox
Illustrations: Matt Ward
Page make-up: Green House Design, Bookham, Surrey

Acknowledgement has been made to Alexander Inglis as the original developer of the Nelson Handwriting script.

Lines from 'Friendly Frederick Fuddlestone' © 1985 Arnold Lobel, reproduced from *Whiskers and Rhymes* by Arnold Lobel by permission of Walker Books Ltd; 'Little Miss Muffett' © Andrea Shavick, reprinted by permission of the author; 'Baked Beans: Special Offer' © Mike Johnson, previously published in *Spotlight on Poetry: What Kind of Poem?* (Collins, 1999), reprinted by permission of the author; 'Pineapple' © John Cotton, reprinted by permission of Mrs Peggy Cotton; 'Fishes in the River' © Valerie Bloom, reprinted by permission of the author; lines from 'Penguins on Ice' © Celia Warren, reprinted by permission of the author.

Nelson Handwriting

Contents

Nelson Handwriting

How to use this book

The *Developing Skills* book provides the core handwriting curriculum for the year. It is differentiated to ensure children can progress through key stages in handwriting at their own pace.

UNIT 16

Practising writing letters with ascenders in proportion.

th

Lightning flickers and thunder crashes.

FOCUS

A Copy this pattern into your book.

B Copy these letters into your book.

th th th th th
ht ht ht ht ht
fl fl fl fl fl

The letters b, d, h, f, k and l all have ascenders. The letter t also has an ascender but it is not as tall.

XTRA

Make these words. Copy them into your book. Remember to slope your writing slightly to the right.

light+ly = lightly light+er = lighter
tight+ly = tightly tight+er = tighter
bright+ly = brightly bright+er = brighter

XTENSION

Copy this poem into your book. Remember to leave the correct space between your letters and between your words.

See lightning is flashing,
The forest is crashing,
The rain will come dashing,
A flood will be rising anon;
The heavens are scowling,
The thunder is growling,
The loud winds are howling,
The storm has come suddenly on!

From 'The Storm' by Sara Coleridge

36 37

There are two copymasters in this book to go with each Unit in the *Developing Skills* book:

The **Focus Resource** is designed for the less-able pupil who needs further practice in the basic teaching point.

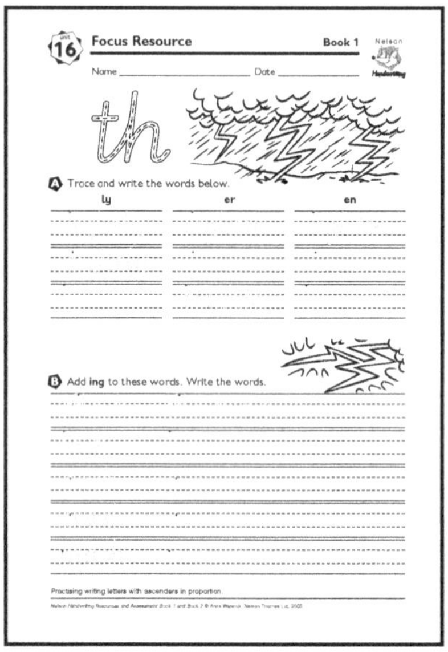
16 Focus Resource Book 1

Name Date

th

A Trace and write the words below.

ly er en

B Add ing to these words. Write the words.

Practising writing letters with ascenders in proportion

The **Extension Resource** caters for the child who needs more demanding work arising from, or linked to, the Unit teaching point.

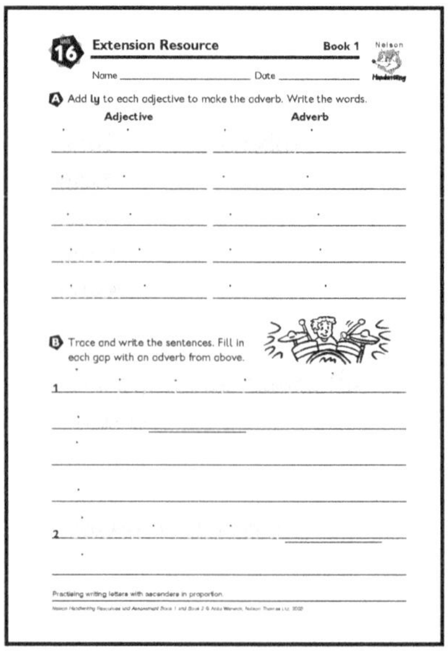
16 Extension Resource Book 1

Name Date

A Add ly to each adjective to make the adverb. Write the words.

Adjective Adverb

B Trace and write the sentences. Fill in each gap with an adverb from above.

1

2

Practising writing letters with ascenders in proportion

Assessment

This book also contains a range of easy-to-administer assessment sheets. These are designed to be used flexibly and come in three forms:

Placement Tests – these can be used at the start of the year to give an overview of a class's handwriting ability. The Tests can be checked against the **LevellingGuide** contained in this book.

The **Handwriting Assessment Record Sheet** is a quick and easy reference tool for the teacher to use to record the level of each child's handwriting.

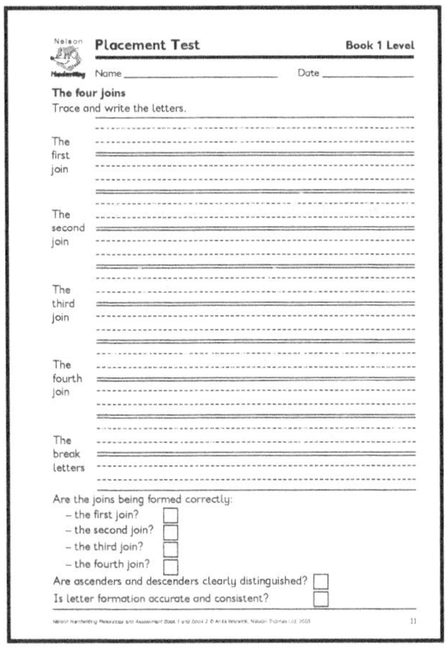

Placement Test   Book 1 Level

Name ______ Date ______

The four joins

Trace and write the letters.

The first join

The second join

The third join

The fourth join

The break letters

Are the joins being formed correctly:
- the first join?
- the second join?
- the third join?
- the fourth join?

Are ascenders and descenders clearly distinguished?

Is letter formation accurate and consistent?

11

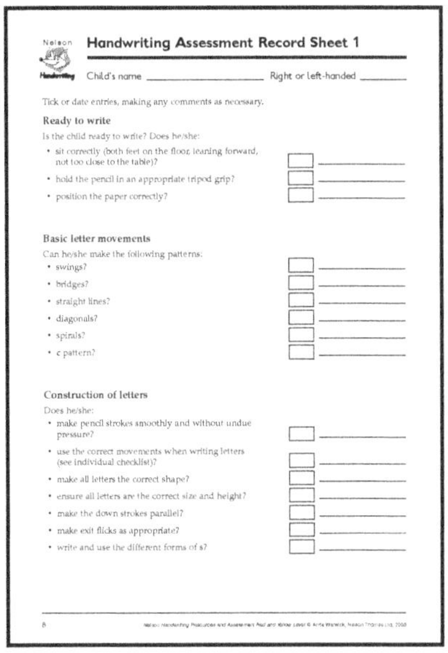

Handwriting Assessment Record Sheet 1

Child's name ______ Right or left-handed ______

Tick or date entries, making any comments as necessary.

Ready to write

Is the child ready to write? Does he/she:
- sit correctly (both feet on the floor, leaning forward, not too close to the table)?
- hold the pencil in an appropriate tripod grip?
- position the paper correctly?

Basic letter movements

Can he/she make the following patterns:
- swings?
- bridges?
- straight lines?
- diagonals?
- spirals?
- c pattern?

Construction of letters

Does he/she:
- make pencil strokes smoothly and without undue pressure?
- use the correct movements when writing letters (see individual checklist)?
- make all letters the correct shape?
- ensure all letters are the correct size and height?
- make the down strokes parallel?
- make exit flicks as appropriate?
- write and use the different forms of s?

8

General Assessment   Book 1 Level

Name ______ Date ______

Joining to and from the letter e

Write this rhyme in your best handwriting in the space below.

The elephant carries a great
big trunk;
He never packs it with clothes;
It has no lock; it has no key,
But he takes it wherever he
goes.

(Anonymous)

Is each letter **e** the correct shape and size?

17

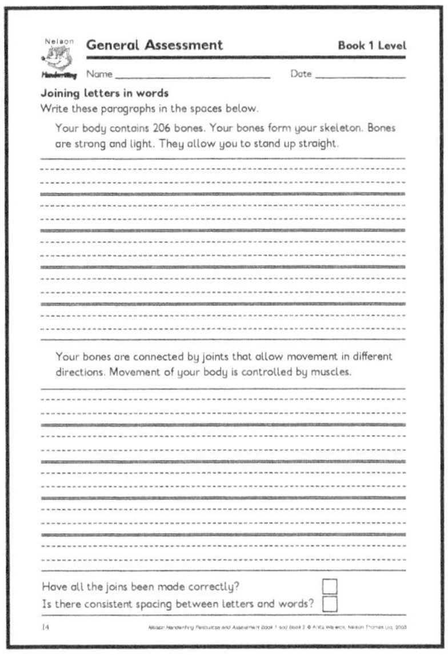

General Assessment   Book 1 Level

Name ______ Date ______

Joining letters in words

Write these paragraphs in the spaces below.

Your body contains 206 bones. Your bones form your skeleton. Bones are strong and light. They allow you to stand up straight.

Your bones are connected by joints that allow movement in different directions. Movement of your body is controlled by muscles.

Have all the joins been made correctly?

Is there consistent spacing between letters and words?

14

Self-assessment Sheets – these reinforce the self-assessment aspect of Nelson Handwriting introduced in the *Workbooks*. The Sheets take pupils through aspects of their handwriting that they need to check. The aim is to help the process become automatic for pupils.

General Assessment Sheets – these are included for each of the main teaching focuses and can be used for extra practice or to check how pupils are coping with the different handwriting challenges.

Also included in this *Resources and Assessment* book are **Guidelines** of the appropriate width, and a helpful left-handed version of the **Getting Ready to Write** flap from the *Developing Skills* books to give to left-handed pupils.

Levelling Guide

For use with **Placement Tests**

These level descriptors should be used alongside the Placement tests in this book. Comparing your pupil's handwriting to the descriptors here will help you place the handwriting ability of your pupils and chart their progress. For more information see page 18 of the Teacher's Book.

England and Wales

Level 1 'Letters are usually clearly shaped and correctly oriented.'

Level 2 'In handwriting, letters are accurately formed and consistent in size.'

Level 3 'Handwriting is joined and legible.'

Level 4 'Handwriting style is fluent, joined and legible.'

Level 5 'Handwriting is joined clear and fluent and, where appropriate, is adapted to a range of tasks.'

Scotland

Level A In writing tasks pupils 'form letters and space words legibly for the most part. At an appropriate stage, linkage of letters will be taught.'

Level B In writing tasks pupils 'form letters and space words legibly in linked script'.

Level C In writing tasks pupils 'employ a fluent, legible style of handwriting'.

Level D In writing tasks pupils 'employ a fluent, legible style of handwriting and set out completed work giving attention to presentation and layout'.

Level E In writing tasks pupils 'employ a fluent, legible style of handwriting, and set out completed work clearly and attractively'.

Northern Ireland

Level 1 'Pupils should show some control over the size, shape and orientation of letters.'

Level 2 'There is evidence of the use of upper and lower case letters.'

Level 3 'Handwriting is accurately formed and consistant in size.'

Level 4 'Handwriting is swift and legible.'

Level 5 'Handwriting is swift and legible.'

Getting ready to write

For use by left-handed pupils

Are you sitting comfortably with both feet on the floor?

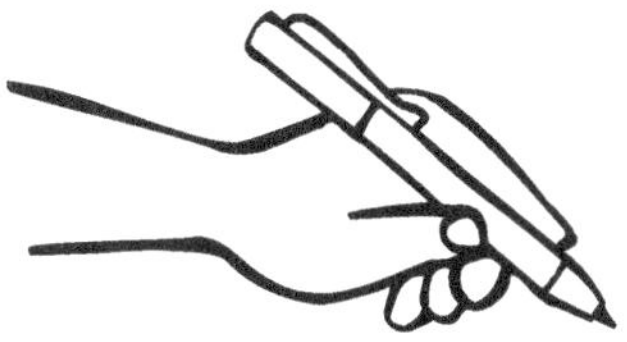

Are you holding your pen correctly?

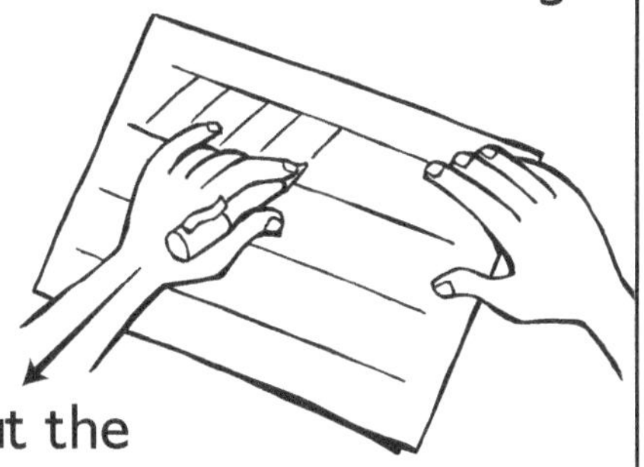

Is your paper at the correct angle?

Nelson Handwriting

Handwriting Assessment Record Sheet 1

Child's name ______________________ Right or left-handed __________

Tick or date entries, making any comments as necessary.

Ready to write

Is the child ready to write? Does he/she:

- sit correctly (both feet on the floor, leaning forward, not too close to the table)? ☐ ______________
- hold the pencil in an appropriate tripod grip? ☐ ______________
- position the paper correctly? ☐ ______________

Basic letter movements

Can he/she make the following patterns:

- swings? ☐ ______________
- bridges? ☐ ______________
- straight lines? ☐ ______________
- diagonals? ☐ ______________
- spirals? ☐ ______________
- c pattern? ☐ ______________

Construction of letters

Does he/she:

- make pencil strokes smoothly and without undue pressure? ☐ ______________
- use the correct movements when writing letters (see individual checklist)? ☐ ______________
- make all letters the correct shape? ☐ ______________
- ensure all letters are the correct size and height? ☐ ______________
- make the down strokes parallel? ☐ ______________
- make exit flicks as appropriate? ☐ ______________
- write and use the different forms of **s**? ☐ ______________

Nelson Handwriting

Handwriting Assessment Record Sheet 2

Child's name ______________________ Right or left-handed __________

Tick or date entries, making any comments as necessary.

The four handwriting joins

Can he/she make the following joins correctly and as one continuous movement:

- the first join – diagonal joins to letters without ascenders? ☐ __________
- the second join – diagonal joins to letters with ascenders? ☐ __________
- the third join – horizontal joins to letters without ascenders? ☐ __________
- the fourth join – horizontal joins to letters with ascenders? ☐ __________

Can he/she:

- use the break letters appropriately and with regular spacing? ☐ __________
- form and join the letter **f** correctly? ☐ __________
- form and join to the letter **e** correctly? ☐ __________

Size and spacing

Is he/she consistent in:

- the size and proportion of letters? ☐ __________
- spacing between letters (letters do not touch)? ☐ __________
- spacing between words? ☐ __________

Presentation

Does he/she:

- use a clear, neat hand in finished, presented work? ☐ __________
- slope writing slightly to the right? ☐ __________
- write fluently and legibly? ☐ __________
- write with speed, e.g. note-taking, lists? ☐ __________
- use informal writing for rough drafting? ☐ __________
- use a range of presentational skills, including: ☐ __________
  - print script for captions, sub headings and labels? ☐ __________
  - decorated borders (as appropriate)? ☐ __________

Guidelines

Levels 1 and 2

Placement Test

Book 1 Level

Name ____________________ Date ____________

The four joins

Trace and write the letters.

The first join

The second join

The third join

The fourth join

The break letters

Are the joins being formed correctly:

- the first join? ☐
- the second join? ☐
- the third join? ☐
- the fourth join? ☐

Are ascenders and descenders clearly distinguished? ☐

Is letter formation accurate and consistent? ☐

Nelson Handwriting

Placement Test

Book 1 Level

Name ______________________ Date ______________

A Trace and write the words.

B Write the sentence.

Hold your pen properly.

Are the letters the correct size and height?	☐
Are the letters formed and joined correctly?	☐
Is there consistent spacing between the letters?	☐

General Assessment

Book 1 Level

Name ______________________ Date ______________

The size and height of letters

A Write these lower-case letters. Make sure they are the correct size and height.

aaa bbb ccc ddd eee fff ggg

hhh iii jjj kkk lll mmm nnn

ooo ppp qqq rrr sss ttt uuu

vvv www xxx yyy zzz

B Write these capital letters to the correct size and height.

A B C D E F G H I J K L M N

O P Q R S T U V W X Y Z

Are the letters the correct size and height? ☐

General Assessment

Book 1 Level

Name ______________________ Date ______________

Joining letters in words

Write these paragraphs in the spaces below.

Your body contains 206 bones. Your bones form your skeleton. Bones are strong and light. They allow you to stand up straight.

Your bones are connected by joints that allow movement in different directions. Movement of your body is controlled by muscles.

Have all the joins been made correctly? ☐

Is there consistent spacing between letters and words? ☐

Nelson Handwriting

General Assessment

Book 1 Level

Name ______________________ Date ____________

Double letters

A Complete these lines.

ff ff

ll ll

ss ss

B Write these words carefully.

cliff cuff off offer raffle

call sell fill bull doll holly

pass boss dress fuss hiss

Are **ff**, **ll** and **ss** joined correctly? ☐

Are letters the correct size and height? ☐

Is there consistent spacing between letters and between words? ☐

Nelson Handwriting

General Assessment

Book 1 Level

Name ______________________ Date ______________

Equal spacing between letters and between words

Write this rhyme in your best handwriting in the space below. Remember to leave a consistent space between your letters *and* a consistent space between your words.

I eat my peas with honey,
I've done it all my life,
It makes the peas taste funny,
But it keeps them on the knife!

(Anonymous)

Do letters have a consistent space between them? ☐

Do words have a consistent space between them? ☐

Do break letters have a consistent space before and after them? ☐

Nelson Handwriting

General Assessment

Book 1 Level

Name ______________________ Date ______________

Joining to and from the letter e

Write this rhyme in your best handwriting in the space below.

The elephant carries a great
big trunk;
He never packs it with clothes;
It has no lock; it has no key,
But he takes it wherever he
goes.

(Anonymous)

Is each letter **e** the correct shape and size? ☐

Nelson Handwriting

General Assessment

Book 1 Level

Name ______________________ Date ______________

Writing letters

Write this letter. Add your school address and the date at the top.

Dear Parents

You are invited to an Open Evening on June 26th. We hope you will come.

Yours sincerely

The Headteacher

Is the letter formatted correctly? ☐

Is the writing neat, fluent and legible? ☐

Self-assessment

Book 1 Level

Name ______________________ Date ______________

A Write this elephant joke in your best handwriting.

Question: Why are elephants so wrinkled?
Answer: Have you ever tried ironing one?

B Write this sentence as quickly as you can three times on a separate sheet of paper.

Six times four add five makes twenty-nine.

	sometimes	*usually*	*always*
Is your handwriting consistent in size?	☐	☐	☐
Is your handwriting joined and legible?	☐	☐	☐
Is your handwriting fluent?	☐	☐	☐

Nelson Handwriting

Self-assessment

Book 1 Level

Name ______________________ Date ______________

Write this poem in the space below. Remember to join your letters and to slope them slightly to the right.

I've never seen a Tudor
They don't live down our street
I've never seen one walking
I've never heard one speak...

I've never ever touched one
They seem so far away
but teacher seems to like them
and we have them every day.

'Tudors' by *Peter Dixon*

	sometimes	*usually*	*always*
Is your handwriting consistent in size?	☐	☐	☐
Is your handwriting joined, sloped and legible?	☐	☐	☐
Is your handwriting fluent?	☐	☐	☐

Nelson Handwriting

Placement Test

Book 2 Level

Name ______________________ Date ______________

Size and height

Write the letters and words.

gggg jjjj yyyy qqqq

goes jumped young queen

vvvv wwww xxxx zzzz vwxz

wax where wives weave zoo

bbbb hhhh kkkk dddd llll

below knew didn't light think

Are the tails or descenders below the line? ☐

Are similar letters the same height? ☐

Are the ascenders on letters the correct height and size? ☐

Nelson Handwriting

Placement Test

Book 2 Level

Name ______________________________ Date __________________

Write this poem in the space below. Remember to slope your writing.

In the dark, dark wood there
was a dark, dark house
And in that dark, dark house
there was a dark, dark room
In that dark, dark room there
was a dark, dark cupboard
And in that dark, dark
cupboard there was a GHOST!

Are the letters and words consistently spaced? ☐

Is the writing evenly sloped? ☐

Nelson Handwriting

General Assessment

Book 2 Level

Name ______________________ Date ______________

Forming and joining letters

A The ovals of **b** and **p** are made in a clockwise direction.
Practise writing these letters.

pool paid upon band bobbing

B Remember, there are two forms of **e**. Practise writing these words.

peep each landed read wave

C Joining **f** and **r** can be difficult. Practice writing these letters and words.

fork friend flour raft flick

D Remember that **s** can change its shape. Practise writing these letters.

stork risk stars rusty frost

Are the letters and words consistently spaced? ☐

Are the letters formed and joined correctly? ☐

Is the writing evenly sloped? ☐

Nelson Handwriting

General Assessment

Book 2 Level

Name ______________________ Date ______________

Joining letters in words

Write these words.

began being brought before

paper place people pool paid

every earth eyes wave read

first following father friends

asked does goes show stopped

started used sometimes still

Are the letters and words consistently spaced? ☐

Are the letters formed and joined correctly? ☐

Is the writing evenly sloped? ☐

Nelson Handwriting

General Assessment

Book 2 Level

Name ______________________ Date ______________

Joining e, f and s correctly

Write these sentences in joined writing. Take care how you join letters to **e**, **f** and **s**.

The fox has very soft fur.

It's better to be safe than sorry.

Beware a wolf in sheep's clothing.

An elephant never forgets.

Has the correct **e** been used? ☐

Has the correct **s** been used? ☐

Is **f** formed and joined correctly? ☐

General Assessment

Name ______________________ Date ______________

Writing quickly, fluently and legibly

A Write this verse as quickly as you can. Make sure your handwriting is fluent and legible.

June brings tulips, lilies, roses,
Fills the children's hands with posies.

B Write this sentence as many times as you can in three minutes on a separate sheet of paper.

August brings the sheaves of corn.

C Divide the total number of letters you wrote by three to find your writing speed.

My writing speed is ____ letters per minute.

Is the writing still legible?	☐
Is the writing sloped to increase speed?	☐
Are the letters the correct size and height?	☐
Are the words and the letter **s** spaced consistently?	☐

General Assessment

Book 2 Level

Name ______________________ Date ______________

Sloped writing

These instructions for washing hair are mixed up. Rewrite them in the correct order. Remember to slope your writing.

- Rub in the shampoo.
- Dry with a towel.
- Wet your hair with warm water.
- Wash until it is clean.
- Rinse off the lather.
- Tip on some shampoo.

1 ______________________

2 ______________________

3 ______________________

4 ______________________

5 ______________________

6 ______________________

Does the writing have an even slope? ☐

Have the letters been formed and joined correctly? ☐

Is there consistent spacing between letters and between words? ☐

Nelson Handwriting

General Assessment

Book 2 Level

Name ______________________ Date ______________

Printing

A This code uses a number for each letter. Write the letters and numbers carefully on a separate sheet using the print letters.

1	2	3	4	5	6	7	8	9	10	11	12	13
a	b	c	d	e	f	g	h	i	j	k	l	m

14	15	16	17	18	19	20	21	22	23	24	25	26
n	o	p	q	r	s	t	u	v	w	x	y	z

B Decode this message. Remember to use print letters.

20 8 9 19   19 5 3 18 5 20

13 5 19 19 1 7 5   3 1 14

2 5   21 14 4 5 18 19 20 15 15 4

9 6   25 15 21   11 14 15 23

20 8 5   3 15 4 5

Are the letters clear and not joined? ☐

Is the use of the print alphabet consistent? ☐

Self-Assessment

Name ______________________________ Date ____________________

Write these paragraphs. Make sure you join all your letters. Leave an equal space between your letters and an equal space between your words.

> There are no active volcanoes in Britain, but there are some extinct ones. Extinct volcanoes are so old that the magma, or molten rock, has stopped trying to force its way to the surface.

	sometimes	usually	always
Is your handwriting consistent in size?	☐	☐	☐
Is your handwriting joined, sloped and legible?	☐	☐	☐
Is your handwriting fluent?	☐	☐	☐

Nelson Handwriting

Self-assessment

Book 2 Level

Name ______________________ Date ______________

Write this poem in the space below. Make sure your writing is sloped slightly to the right.

I can get through a doorway
without any key,
And strip the leaves
from the great oak tree.
I can drive storm clouds
and shake tall towers,
Or steal through a garden
and not wake the flowers.

From ***'The Wind'*** by *James Reeves*

	sometimes	*usually*	*always*
Is your handwriting consistent in size?	☐	☐	☐
Is your handwriting joined, sloped and legible?	☐	☐	☐
Is your handwriting fluent?	☐	☐	☐

unit 1

Focus Resource

Book 1

Nelson Handwriting

Name ______________________ Date ________________

A Trace and write the pattern and letters.

B Trace and write the words and the sentence.

Practising writing descenders.

Extension Resource

Book 1

Nelson Handwriting

Name ______________________ Date ______________

A Trace and write the letters and words.

B Trace and write the sentence.

Practising writing descenders.

Focus Resource

Book 1

Nelson Handwriting

Name ____________________ Date ______________

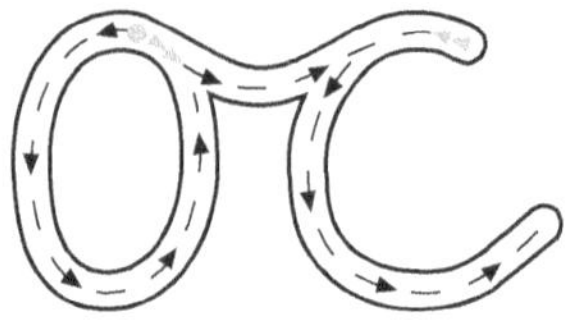

A Trace and write the pattern and letters.

B Trace and write the words.

knock

clock

nod

rod

moon

spoon

Practising joining from the letter **o**.

Extension Resource

Name ______________________ Date ______________

A Trace and write the question.

What did the wolf say?

B Choose the answer from the box and write it under the question.

Practising joining from the letter **o**.

Focus Resource

Name ______________________ Date ______________

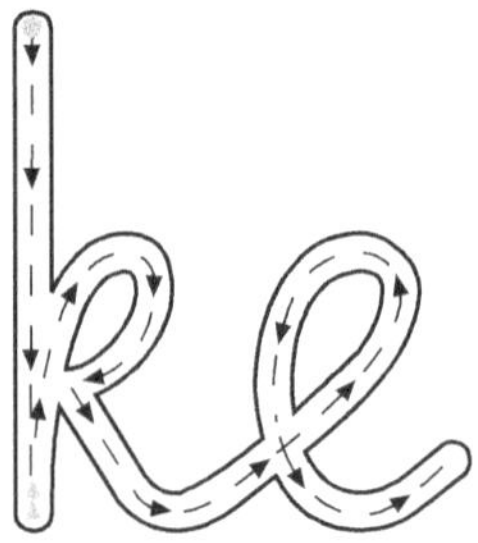

A Trace and write the pattern and letters.

eee eee

ke ke

B Trace and write the words.

cake

lake

dome

home

hare

share

Practising joining to the letter **e**.

Extension Resource

Book 1

Nelson Handwriting

Name ______________________________ Date ____________________

A Verbs ending in **e** drop the **e** when **ing** is added.
Trace and write the words.

take taking

B Add **ing** to these words. Trace and write the words.

Practising joining to the letter **e**.

Focus Resource

Nelson Handwriting

Name ______________________ Date ______________

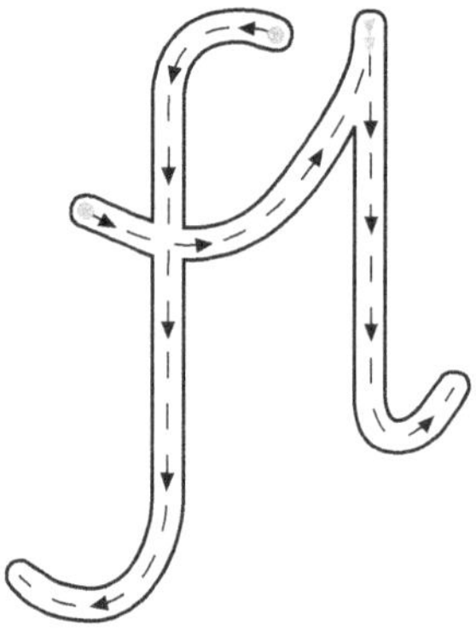

A Trace and write the pattern and letters.

B Trace and write the words.

flan

flannel

flower

flee

fleece

Practising joining to the letter **l**.

Extension Resource

Book 1

Nelson Handwriting

Name ______________________ Date ______________

A Homonyms are words that have two meanings.
Trace and write the words.

B Trace and write the sentences. Fill in each gap with the correct word from above.

1

2

Practising joining to the letter **l**.

Focus Resource

Book 1

Name ______________________ Date ______________

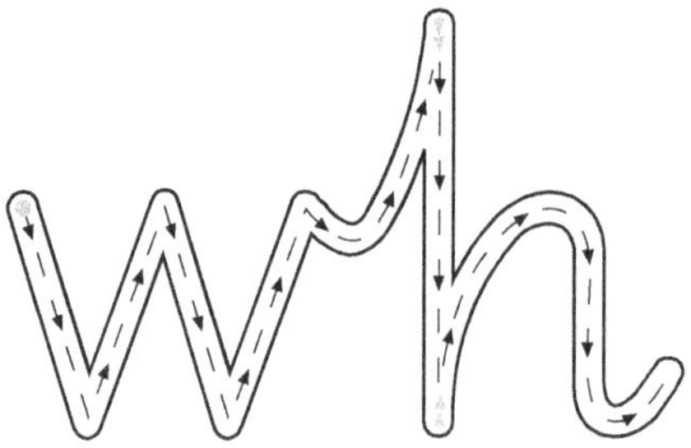

A Trace and write the pattern and letters.

ww ww

wh wh

wh wh

wh wh

B Trace and write the words.

white

wherever

whale

what

wheel

when

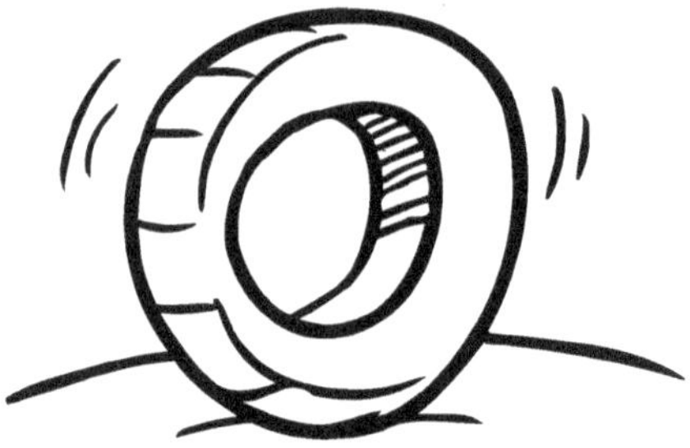

Practising joining from the letter **w**.

unit 5

Extension Resource

Book 1

Name ______________________ Date ______________

A Trace and write the letters and words.

B Trace and write the sentences. Fill in each gap with the correct word from above.

1 ______________________

2 ______________________

3 ______________________

Practising joining from the letter **w**.

unit 6

Focus Resource

Book 1

Nelson Handwriting

Name ______________________ Date ________________

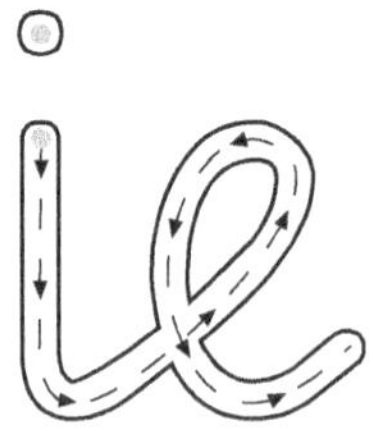

A Trace and write the pattern and letters.

B Trace and write the words.

Practising joining from the letter **i**.

unit 6

Extension Resource

Book 1

Nelson Handwriting

Name ______________________ Date ______________

A Trace and write the words.

B Trace and write the sentence. Fill in the gap with the correct word from above.

Practising joining from the letter **i**.

Focus Resource

Name ______________________ Date ________________

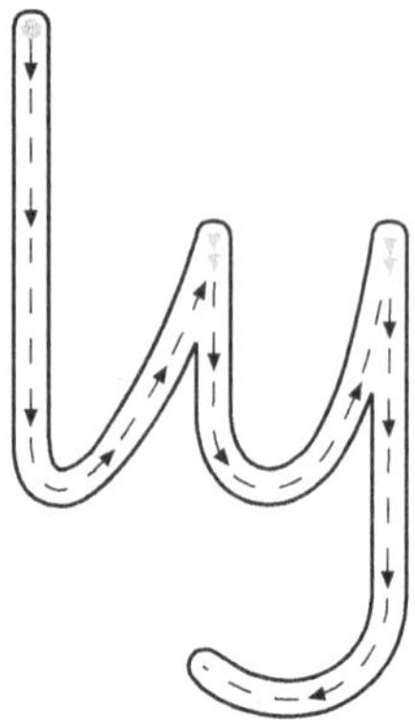

A Trace and write the pattern and letters.

B Trace and write the words.

Practising diagonal joins to the letter **y**.

Extension Resource

unit 7 **Book 1**

Nelson Handwriting

Name ______________________ Date ______________

A Add **ly** or **ny** to these words. Trace and write the words.

B Trace and write the sentence.

Practising diagonal joins to the letter **y**.

Focus Resource

Book 1

Nelson Handwriting

Name ______________________ Date ______________

ap

A Trace and write the pattern and letters.

B Trace and write the words.

approve

disapprove

arrange

disarrange

allow

disallow

Practising joining from the letter **a**.

unit 8

Extension Resource

Book 1

Nelson Handwriting

Name ______________________ Date ______________

A Add the prefix **un** to these words. Trace and write the words.

B Trace and write the sentences. Fill in each gap with the correct word from above.

1 ______________________

2 ______________________

Practising joining from the letter **a**.

Nelson Handwriting

Name ____________________ Date ______________

A Trace and write the pattern and letters.

ckck ckck

ckck ckck

B Trace and write the words.

brick

chick

buckle

chuckle

black

crack

Practising joining to the letter **k**.

Extension Resource

unit 9

Book 1

Nelson Handwriting

Name ______________________ Date ______________

A Trace and write this informal letter.

Dear Jack,

me to your sports party

B Now sign the letter.

Practising joining to the letter **k**.

Focus Resource

Name ______________________ Date ______________

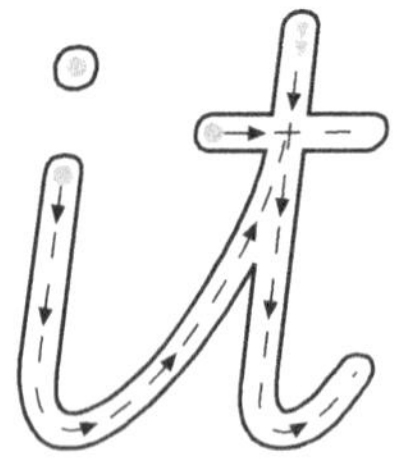

A Trace and write the pattern and letters.

B Trace and write the words.

Practising writing with a slope.

unit 10

Extension Resource

Book 1

Nelson Handwriting

Name ______________________ Date ______________

A Trace and write the weather rhyme. Try to slope your writing slightly to the right.

B Look at your writing. Does it slope slightly to the right? If not, try writing this word.

C Use your ruler to check your downstrokes are parallel and your writing is sloping slightly to the right.

Practising writing with a slope.

unit 11

Focus Resource

Book 1

Nelson Handwriting

Name ______________________ Date ______________

he

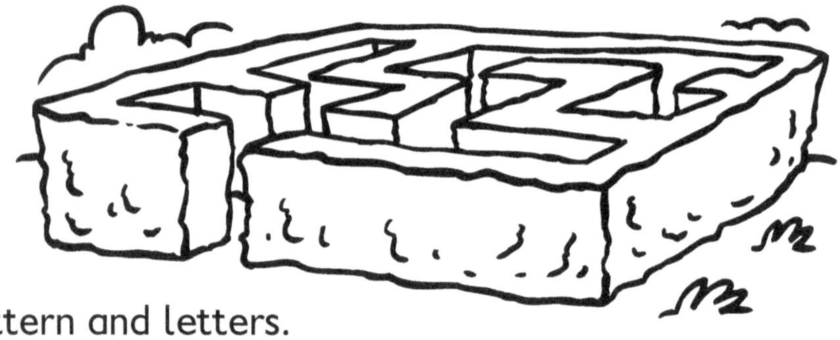

A Trace and write the pattern and letters.

nene nene

he he

re re

B Trace and write the words.

heavy

heavier

weaken

weakest

strength

strengthen

Practising joining to the letter **e**.

Extension Resource

Name ______________________ Date ______________

These words are contractions.

she's	you've	I've	we'll
they've	we're	you're	he'll

Trace and write the words. Write in the correct contraction from above.

Contraction

Practising joining to the letter **e**.

unit 12

Focus Resource

Book 1

Nelson Handwriting

Name ______________________ Date ______________

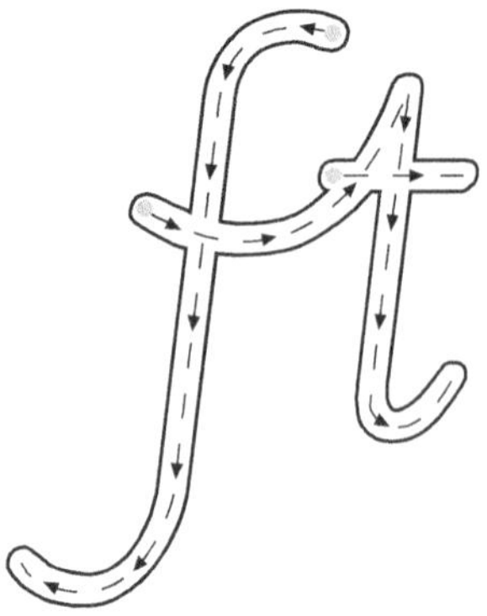

A Trace and write the pattern and letters.

B Trace and write the words.

after

afterwards

after all

finish

first

finally

Practising joining from the letter **f**.

Extension Resource

Book 1

Nelson Handwriting

Name ______________________ Date ______________

Trace and write the sentence.

Friendly Frederick

Fuddlestone

From ***'Friendly Frederick Fuddlestone'*** by *Arnold Lobel*

Practising joining from the letter **f**.

unit 13

Focus Resource

Book 1

Nelson Handwriting

Name ______________________ Date ________________

wr

Choose one of the words to match each picture. Write the word in the space. Write the silent letter in the box.

kneel knit knife knead knock

wreck wren writing gnome

Practising writing silent letters.

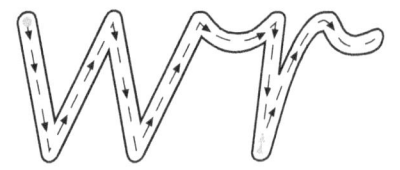

Unit 13 Extension Resource

Book 1

Nelson Handwriting

Name ______________________ Date ______________

A Trace and write the words.

B Write each word from above in the correct column.

wre	kne	wro

Practising writing silent letters.

Focus Resource

Name ______________________ Date ______________

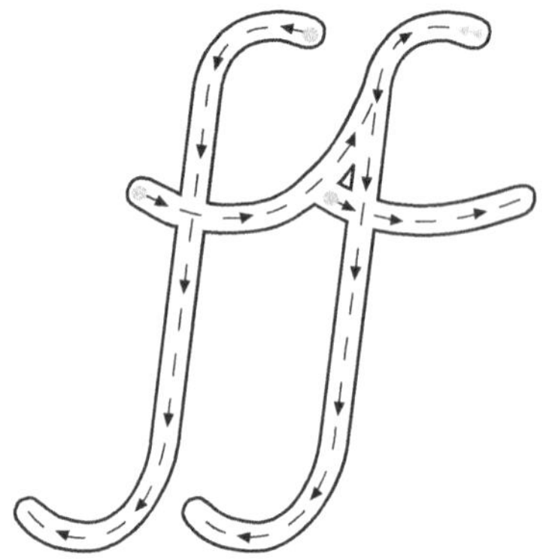

A Trace and write the pattern and letters.

B Trace and write the words.

saddle

poodle

handle

kettle

Practising forming double letters correctly.

Extension Resource

unit 14 | **Book 1** | Nelson Handwriting

Name ______________________ Date ______________

hugging knitting gripping
cuddling rubbing stirring

Trace and write the list poem. Fill in each gap with a word from above.

Practising forming double letters correctly.

Focus Resource

Name ______________________ Date ______________

ew

A Trace and write the pattern and letters.

ewew ewew

ew ew

ev ev

ex ex

B Trace and write the words.

view

preview

event

prevent

exit

exchange

Practising spacing letters consistently.

unit 15

Extension Resource

Book 1

Nelson Handwriting

Name ______________________ Date ________________

Trace and write the poem.

Little Miss Muffet

By *Andrea Shavick*

Practising spacing letters consistently.

unit 16

Focus Resource

Book 1

Nelson Handwriting

Name ______________________ Date ______________

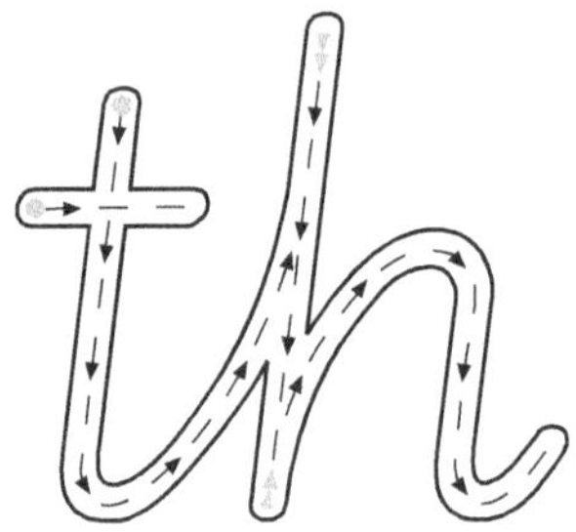

A Trace and write the words below.

ly	er	en
lightly	lighter	lighten

B Add **ing** to these words. Write the words.

flash flashing

Practising writing letters with ascenders in proportion.

Extension Resource

unit 16 — **Book 1** — Nelson Handwriting

Name ______________________ Date ______________

A Add **ly** to each adjective to make the adverb. Write the words.

Adjective	**Adverb**
loud	loudly

B Trace and write the sentences. Fill in each gap with an adverb from above.

1 ______________________________

____

2 ______________________________

____

Practising writing letters with ascenders in proportion.

Focus Resource

Book 1

Name ______________________ Date ______________

ac

A Trace and write the pattern and letters.

acac acac

ac ac

B Trace and write the words.

pack

back

cage

page

raft

daft

Practising joining from the letter **a**.

Extension Resource

Book 1

Nelson Handwriting

Name ______________________ Date ________________

These instructions for making a jam sandwich have got mixed up.
Write the sentences in the correct order.
Remember to leave a consistent space between your letters and words.

•

•

•

•

•

Practising joining from the letter **a**.

unit 18

Focus Resource

Book 1

Nelson Handwriting

Name ______________________ Date ______________

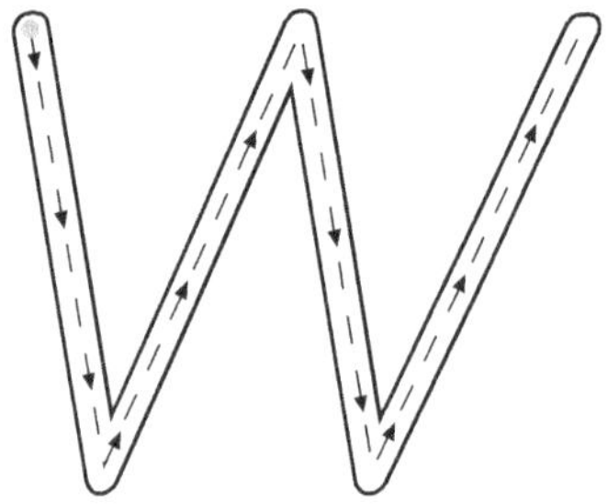

A Trace and write the pattern and letters.

B Write your name and address. Put capital letters in the correct places.

Practising forming capital letters.

unit 18

Extension Resource

Book 1

Nelson Handwriting

Name ______________________ Date ________________

Trace the poem.

BAKED BEANS: SPECIAL OFFER

By *Mike Johnson*

Focus Resource

Name ______________________ Date ________________

Copy the decorated capital letters.

Name ______________________ Date ______________

Trace the poem. Make the letters M, A, B and W into decorated capital letters.

PINEAPPLE

By *John Cotton*

Practising writing decorated capital letters.

unit 20

Focus Resource

Book 1

Nelson Handwriting

Name ____________________ Date ______________

A Trace and write the questions. Write your own answer underneath.

1 How old are you?

2 Which school do you go to?

3 Where do you live?

4 How do you get to school?

Practising with punctuation.

Extension Resource

unit 20 **Book 1** Nelson Handwriting

Name ______________________ Date ______________

Trace and write the sentences. Put in the speech marks.

Practising with punctuation.

unit 1

Focus Resource

Book 2

Nelson Handwriting

Name ______________________ Date ______________

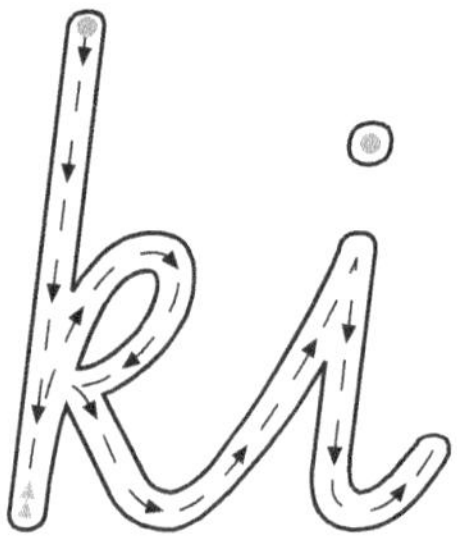

A Trace and write the pattern and letters.

B Trace and write the words.

carry

marry

hollow

letter

daddy

Practising consistency in size and proportion of letters.

Extension Resource

Name ______________________ Date ______________

Copy the passage.

Erik was a

Viking warrior. His ship was

called the Golden Dragon. The

ship's figurehead was a fierce

monster carved out of wood

and covered with gold leaf.

Practising consistency in size and proportion of letters.

unit 2

Focus Resource

Book 2

Nelson Handwriting

Name ______________________ Date ______________

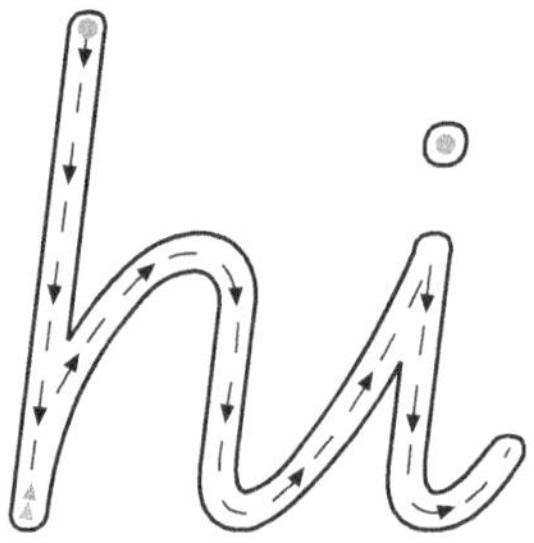

A Trace and write the pattern and letters.

B Trace and write the words.

membership

enjoyment

silliness

careless

thankless

Practising using a diagonal joining line.

Extension Resource

Name ______________________________ Date __________________

A suffix such as **ship**, **hood** or **ness** appears at the end of a word.
Copy this sentence. Choose the correct word.

Legend has it that King

Alfred was so busy thinking

about fighting that he

burned some cakes in a fit of

(absent minded/

absent mindedness).

Practising using a diagonal joining line.

Focus Resource

Book 2

Nelson Handwriting

Name ______________________ Date ______________

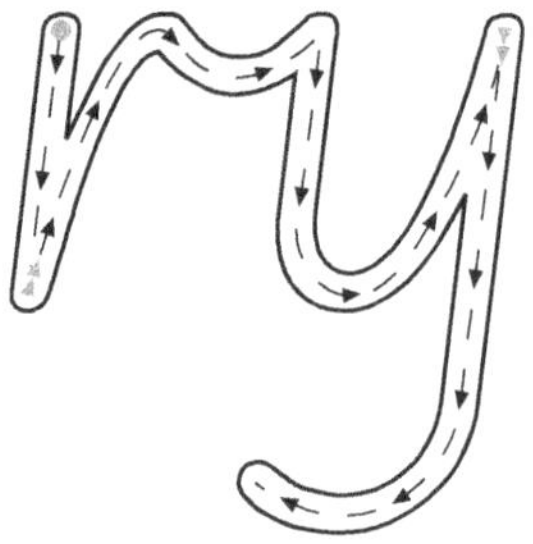

A Trace and write the pattern and letters.

B Trace and write the words.

February

stationery

laundry

foundry

Practising leaving an equal space between letters.

Extension Resource

Book 2

Nelson Handwriting

Name ______________________ Date ______________

A Copy the words.

library

stationary

dictionary

B Copy the sentence. Fill in the gap with the correct word from above.

The plane was ______________

on the runway for an hour

before it took off.

Practising leaving an equal space between letters.

Focus Resource

Book 2

Nelson Handwriting

Name ______________________ Date ______________

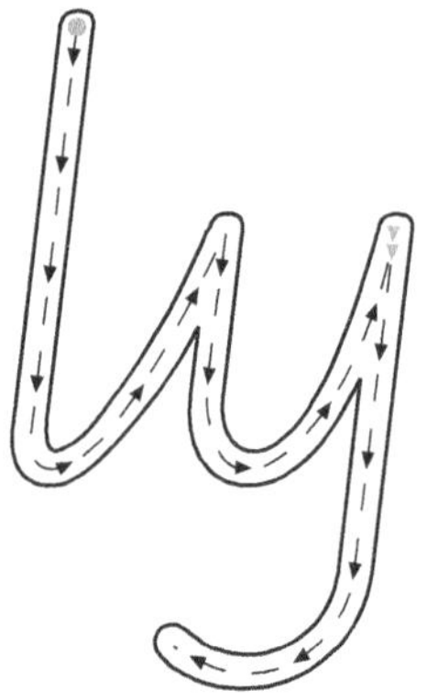

A Trace and write the pattern and letters.

B Trace and write the words.

Practising joining to the letter **y**.

Extension Resource

unit 4 — Book 2 — Nelson Handwriting

Name ______________________ Date ______________

A Copy the words.

pure purify

speed speedily

terror terrify

B Copy the sentences. Fill in each gap with the correct word from above.

1 People can ride bicycles to

move around ____________.

2 The water in many rivers

is not ____________.

Practising joining to the letter **y**.

Focus Resource

Nelson Handwriting

Name ______________________ Date ________________

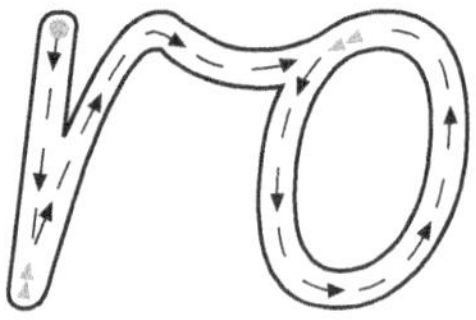

A Trace and write the pattern and letters.

roro roro

B Trace and write the words.

rowdy

nowadays

howl

bowl

rainbow

Practising using a horizontal joining line.

Extension Resource

Name ____________________ Date ______________

These are present-tense words.

ring blow sing take fight
sell tell have shake buy

These are past-tense words.

blew rang sang sold told had
took shook fought bought

Match each past-tense word to its present-tense word.
Write the pairs of words.

Present	Past	Present	Past
blow	blew		took

unit 6

Focus Resource

Book 2

Nelson Handwriting

Name ______________________ Date ______________

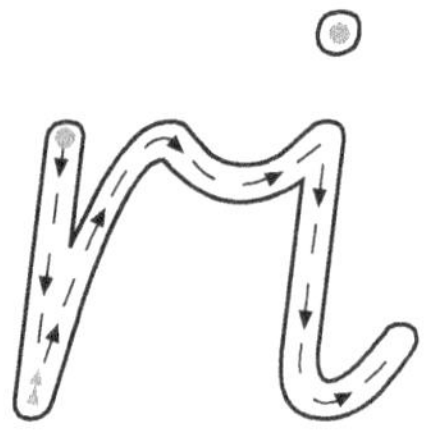

A Trace and write the pattern and letters.

B Trace and write the words.

married

hurried

worried

marries

hurries

worries

Practising the size and height of letters.

Extension Resource

Book 2

Name ______________________ Date ______________

Most words add **s**, **ed** or **ing** to show tenses. Fill in the correct words.

	s	ed	ing
cook	cooks	cooked	cooking
book			
stay			
play			

With short vowels, double the final consonant before adding **ed** or **ing**.

	ed	ing
hop	hopped	hopping
stop		
drop		

If a word ends in **e**, avoid **ee** by dropping one **e**.

	s	ed
save	saves	saved
pave		
wave		

Practising the size and height of letters.

Focus Resource

Name ______________________ Date ________________

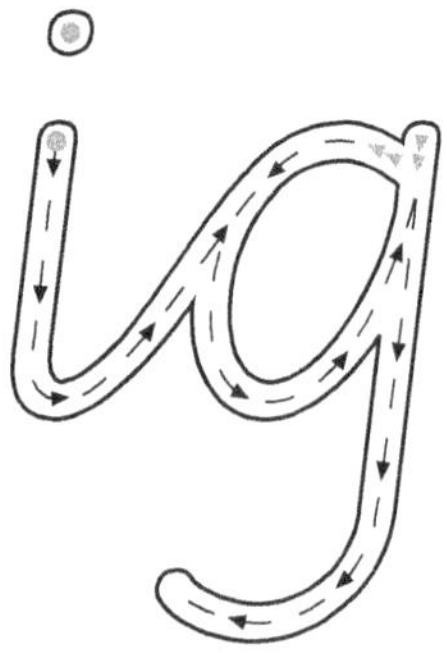

A Trace and write the pattern.

B Add **ight** to make the words. Write the new words.

C Use one of the words from above in a sentence.

Practising joining from the letter **i**.

unit 7

Extension Resource

Book 2

Nelson Handwriting

Name ______________________ Date ______________

A Most words ending in the 'ight' sound use **ight**. A handful of words use **ite**. Copy the words.

night	white
knight	bite
fight	rite
slight	mite

B Copy the sentences. Fill in each gap with the correct word from above.

1 Snow is ______________.

2 The ____________ grasped his sword and began to ____________.

Practising joining from the letter **i**.

unit 8

Focus Resource

Book 2

Nelson Handwriting

Name ______________________ Date ________________

ive

A Trace and write the pattern.

B Add **ive** or **tive** to make the words. Write the new words.

C Use one of the words from above in a sentence.

Practising joining to and from the letter **v**.

unit 8

Extension Resource

Book 2

Nelson Handwriting

Name ______________________ Date ______________

A Copy the words.

massive

relative

competitive

expensive

B Copy the sentences. Fill in each gap with the correct word from above.

1 I built a __________ tower with all the bricks in the box.

2 The magician made the __________ watch disappear.

Practising joining to and from the letter **v**.

Focus Resource

Name ______________________ Date ________________

ar

A Trace and write the pattern and letters.

B Trace and write the words.

Practising consistency in forming and joining letters.

unit 9

Extension Resource

Book 2

Nelson Handwriting

Name ____________________ Date ______________

A Copy the words.

see · meet ·

week · feet ·

tee · leek ·

seem · flee ·

reed · been ·

peel · reel ·

B Change the **ee** in each word to **ea**. Write the new words.

sea ·

C Write a sentence containing 'sea' and 'see'.

Practising consistency in forming and joining letters.

Focus Resource

Nelson Handwriting

Name ______________________ Date ______________

A Write the sentence quickly. Make sure your writing is easy to read.

Leave wild flowers to grow

so that other people may

enjoy them too.

B Look carefully at your letters and joins. Are they correct? Write the sentence again and see if you can improve your writing.

C Check your writing again. Practise on spare paper until you can write the sentence quickly and accurately.

Practising speedwriting.

Extension Resource

Name ______________________ Date ______________

A Copy this passage quickly but neatly.

The tallest living animal in the world is the giraffe. The longest animal ever recorded is the bootlace worm. One of these worms was washed ashore in Scotland. People could not believe its length.

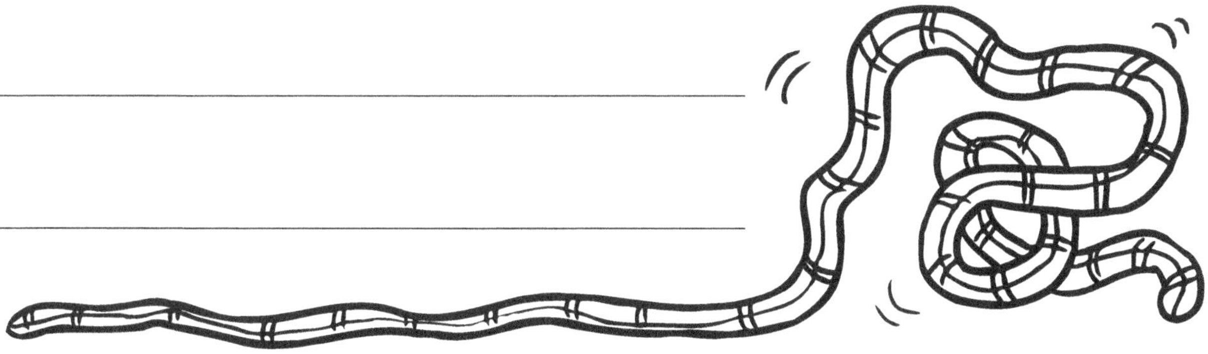

B Now time yourself. To find out your writing speed, count the letters and divide them by the number of minutes.

My writing speed is ______________

letters per minute.

Practising speedwriting.

Focus Resource

Name ______________________ Date ______________

A Trace and write the pattern and letters.

ttt ttt

att att

B Trace and write the words.

hotter

jotter

flutter

potter

blotter

butter

spotter

Practising crossing double **tt** on completing the word.

Extension Resource

Name ______________________ Date ______________

Copy the poem. Remember to cross the double **tt** when you have finished writing the word.

WHAT SOME PEOPLE DO

Chatter, patter, tattle, prattle,

Chew the rag and crack,

Spell and spout and spit it

out, Tell the world and quack.

(Anonymous)

Practising crossing double **tt** on completing the word.

unit 12

Focus Resource

Book 2

Nelson Handwriting

Name ______________________ Date ______________

A Trace and write the pattern and letters.

B Nouns ending in **fe** or **f** change to **ves** when plural.
Trace and write the words.

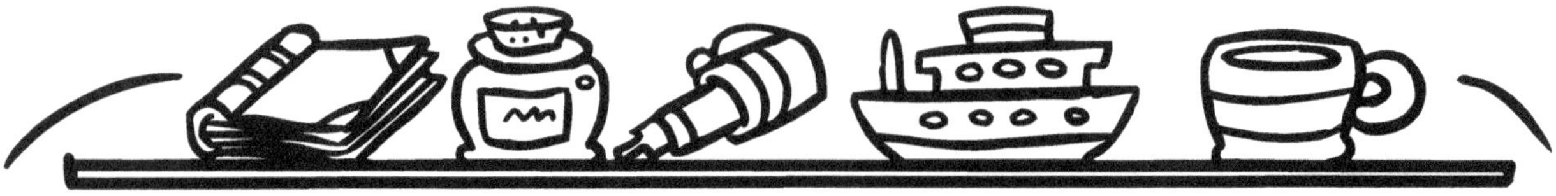

Practising joining to and from the letter **e**.

Extension Resource

Name ______________________ Date ________________

Copy the poem.

FISHES IN THE RIVER

Fishes in the river,

Fishes in the sea,

Fishes in the saucepan,

Fishes for my tea.

By *Valerie Bloom*

Practising joining to and from the letter **e**.

Focus Resource

Book 2

Nelson Handwriting

Name ______________________ Date ______________

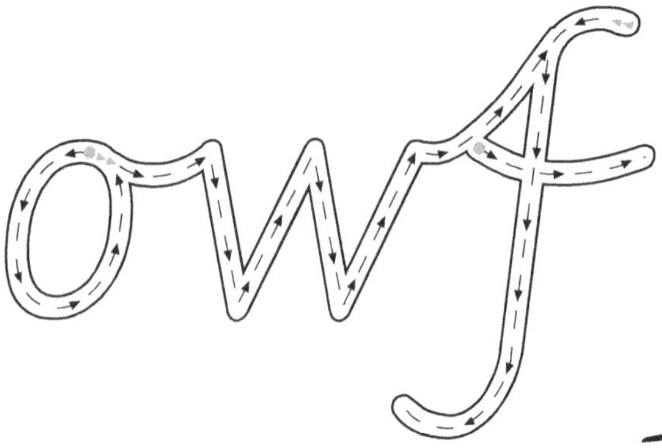

A Trace and write the pattern.

B Trace and write the words.

Practising joining to and from the letter **w**.

Extension Resource

Name ______________________________ Date ___________________

A This three-line poem is called a haiku. Write the haiku on a sheet of paper.

Geese flock heading south
Flying in a v-shaped line
Escaping winter

B A cinquain has five lines. Write this cinquain on a sheet of paper.

Blizzards
Outside – icy
Dangerous for travel
Inside – so very much warmer
We'll stay

C Make up a cinquain and present it on a sheet of paper.

Practising joining to and from the letter **w**.

unit 14

Focus Resource

Book 2

Nelson Handwriting

Name ______________________ Date ______________

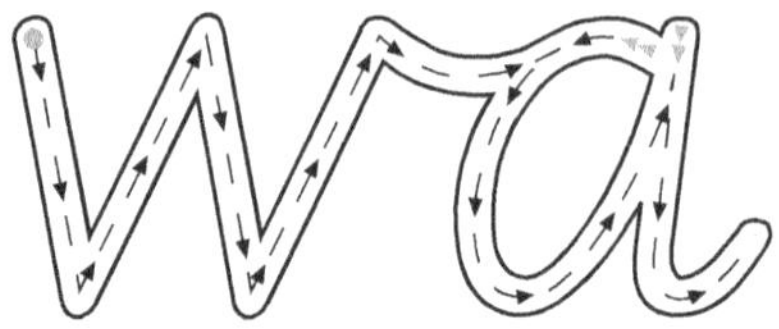

A Trace and write the pattern.

B Trace and write the words.

C Use one of the words from above in a sentence.

Practising joining to the letter **a** from the letter **w**.

Extension Resource

Book 2

Nelson Handwriting

Name ______________________ Date ______________

A Copy the words.

swallow

water

reward

B Copy the sentences. Fill in each gap with the correct word from above.

1 Well done! Here is a ____________.

2 The thirsty dog tried to ____________ too much ____________.

Practising joining to the letter **a** from the letter **w**.

Focus Resource

Name ______________________ Date ______________

Detectives often need to write quick notes. Later they write their report from the notes. Write the meaning of these notes. The first one is done to help you.

Meaning

At 12.30 I see Fingers Smith.

Practising speedwriting.

Extension Resource

Book 2

Nelson Handwriting

Name ______________________ Date ________________

When a pizza restaurant takes orders over the phone, the waiter has to make quick notes. Note down these pizza orders in your quickest handwriting.

My name is Mrs Davies, 17 High Street. Please deliver six pizzas: one with tomatoes, cheese and mushrooms; three with pepperoni, olives, cheese and garlic; and two with, bacon, egg and tomatoes.

My name is Mr Aziz, 33 Southampton Street. I would like three pizzas: two with anchovies, olives, tomatoes and cheese and one with salami, mushrooms, tomatoes and peppers.

Practising speedwriting.

Focus Resource

Book 2

Nelson Handwriting

Name ______________________ Date ______________

Use print to write the labels in the correct places on this street plan. Make the labels as neat as you can.

North Street   South Street   West Street   East Street

Victoria Park   Nelson's Bank   Town Hall   Post Office

Western Stores   Eastward School

Practising printing.

Extension Resource

Book 2

Nelson Handwriting

Name ______________________ Date ______________

Use print to write the names of the cities in the correct places on this map.

Oslo Stockholm Glasgow Dublin London Berlin
Warsaw Paris Vienna Madrid Rome Athens

Practising printing.

Focus Resource

Name ______________________ Date ______________

Tom has written the first draft of the beginning of a story. Many of the spellings are wrong. Write a neat copy and correct the spellings.

Sam and I desidid to explor the old house. We walkt up the frunt parth. The door creeked when we pusht it. The house was all darck inside. We felt a bit fritened.

Practising drafting and editing.

unit 17

Extension Resource

Book 2

Nelson Handwriting

Name ______________________ Date ______________

Emma has written the first draft of the beginning of a story. She has started to edit it, crossing out the words she wants to change. Write a neat copy. Choose words to replace the ones that are crossed out.

Donald had always ~~loved~~ dogs. Dogs were in his all time top ~~10~~ animals list, closely followed by ~~Snakes~~ and Polar Bears. But this dog was special. ~~It~~ had followed him home one day and no matter how many steps he took, it trotted behind him. The dog was ~~ginger~~ and when ~~it~~ panted ~~it~~ looked like ~~it~~ was laughing. Donald ~~loved~~ this dog.

unit 18

Focus Resource

Book 2

Nelson Handwriting

Name ______________________ Date ______________

When you need to write quickly, use numerals instead of number words.

A Write the numerals as fast as you can.

11 12 13 14 15

16 17 18 19 20

B Write the number words as fast as you can.

eleven twelve

thirteen fourteen

fifteen

sixteen seventeen

eighteen

nineteen

twenty

Practising speedwriting.

Extension Resource

unit 18 | **Book 2** | Nelson Handwriting

Name ______________________ Date ______________

Reporters have to write quickly. They often use notes. This is a reporter's finished article.

A Underline the main points in the article.

I ARRIVED AT THE SCENE of the fire at 10 o'clock at 15 Brookside. The fire brigade arrived at 10.05. At 10.06 I saw flames coming through the roof. A woman appeared at an upstairs window and screamed. By 10.08 the firefighters were using water hoses on the fire. A crowd had gathered. At 10.10 a ladder went up and a firefighter climbed it. At 10.12 he reached the upstairs window. Flames appeared behind the woman. At 10.13 the firefighter carried the woman down. She was put in an ambulance and taken to the QE II hospital.

B Now finish the notes from which the article was written.

10.00 Arr. at fr. 15 Brksd.

10.05 Fr. bdgd. arr.

Practising speedwriting.

unit 19

Focus Resource

Book 2

Nelson Handwriting

Name ____________________ Date ______________

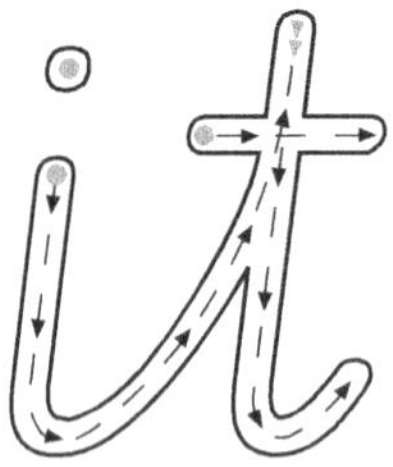

A Trace and write the words.

it's = it is

its = belonging to it

B Trace and write the sentences. Fill in each gap with the correct word from above.

1

on the gate

2 Hurry up, ____ a lovely day

Practising joining to the letter **t**.

Extension Resource

unit 19 — Book 2 — Nelson Handwriting

Name ______________________ Date ______________

Copy the poem. Remember to cross the letter **t** when you have finished writing the word.

Every penguin's mum

can toboggan on her tum.

She can only do that

as she's fluffy and fat:

It must be nice

to live on ice.

From ***Penguins on Ice*** by *Celia Warren*

Practising joining to the letter **t**.

unit 20

Focus Resource

Book 2

Nelson Handwriting

Name ______________________ Date ______________

A Write the print alphabet and the numerals as neatly as you can.

B Now look at your writing. If you are not happy with it, practise on spare paper.

Practising printing.

Extension Resource

Book 2

Nelson Handwriting

Name ______________________ Date ______________

Rachel and Daniel saw this poster in the travel agent's window. Copy the poster neatly. Remember to use print letters.

Practising printing.

Guidelines

Levels 1 and 2